The 'ed' Shed
VI

By Viola & Zaida Stefano

VeeZee Publications

Copyright © VeeZee Publications Pty. Ltd. 2025

First published in Australia in 2025
by VeeZee Publications Pty. Ltd.

veezeepublications.com

The right of Viola Stefano to be identified as the author of this work have been asserted by her in accordance with the **Copyright Amendment (Moral Rights) Act 2000.**

All rights reserved. Apart from any use as permitted by the author & under the **Copyright Act 1968**, no part may be reproduced, copied, scanned, stored in a retrieval system, recorded, or shared, by any means or in any form, without prior written & signed authorization from the publisher.

ISBN: 978-1-923120-23-5

A catalogue record of this book is available from the **National Library of Australia.**

Author: Viola Stefano
Illustrations, cover & internal designs: Zaida Stefano

Illustrations copyright © Zaida Stefano 2025
Design copyright © Zaida Stefano 2025

Disclaimer: The content presented in this book is meant for educational purposes only. The author & publisher claim no accountability to any entity or person for any liability, damage, or loss caused or assumed to be caused directly or indirectly as a consequence of the application, use, or interpretation of the material in this book.

Core words used in this book

I	**want**	**can**	stop	look
like	more	**he**	go	**see**
here	what	do	**the**	**and**
out	where	we	**it**	up
not	they	when	that	down
she	now	them	**is**	put
help	**off**	you	yes	**on**
turn	who	this	no	why
done	make	**a**	**to**	under
come	**in**	some	which	there
open	get	good	same	home

Ted sits on his little red bed.

He can see a big red shed.

Ted can see a little red sled.

It is in the big red shed.

Ted can see the cat called Zed.

Zed is in the big red shed.

Zed sits on the little red sled.

She is waiting to be fed.

Ted jumps off his little red bed.

He walks to the big red shed.

Ted and Zed want to be fed.

Words that end in 'ed' in this book

Ted	Zed	bed
red	shed	fed
	sled	

We hope you had fun reading!

Learning made easy with VeeZee

VeeZee Publications

Wait, there's more!

Visit our website for information about our range of readers & supporting products.

veezeepublications.com

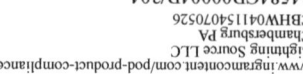